PRAYING
FOR THE
PRODIGAL

Encouragement and Practical Advice
While Waiting for the Prodigal to Return

Andrea Merrell

Straight Street Books
Lighthouse Publishing of the Carolinas

PRAYING FOR THE PRODIGAL BY ANDREA MERRELL
Published by Straight Street Books
An imprint of Lighthouse Publishing of the Carolinas
2333 Barton Oaks Dr., Raleigh, NC 27614

ISBN 978-1-941103-79-1

Copyright © 2015 by Andrea Merrell
Cover design by Goran Tomic
Interior Design by AtriTeX Technologies P Ltd

Available in print from your local bookstore, online, or from the publisher at:
www.lighthousepublishingofthecarolinas.com

For more information on this book and the author visit: www.andreamerrell.com.

Brought to you by the creative team at LighthousePublishingoftheCarolinas.com: Eddie Jones, Amberlyn Dwinnell, Jessica Everson, and Cindy Sproles.

Library of Congress Cataloging-in-Publication Data
Merrell, Andrea
Praying for the Prodigal/ Andrea Merrell 1st ed.

Printed in the United States of America

PRAISE FOR *PRAYING FOR THE PRODIGAL*

A must-read for every parent, *Praying for the Prodigal* is a powerful little book. Andrea's writing is both conversational and compelling. As I read her personal story of her own prodigals, I was deeply touched. Her book is full of reality—no sugar-coating the truth of what can happen when the world gets ahold of our children—but it's also full of hope and healing, showing the restoration that only God can bring. *Praying for the Prodigal* is so relevant and needed today, and I know that every person who reads this book will walk away with restored hope and renewed strength. I certainly did. Kudos to Andrea!

~ **Michelle Medlock Adams**
Award-winning author of fifty-nine books

Of all the parenting books I've read, few have given me more hope than this one. Andrea's personal story of being the parent of two prodigals is an amazing testimony to God's faithfulness and the power of prayer. Too, out of her own experience, Andrea is able to share practical lessons in dealing with prodigal children and praying them home. I highly recommend *Praying for the Prodigal* for all parents longing to see their children in a right relationship with God.

~ **Ann Tatlock**
Award-winning novelist and children's book author

As the mom of a prodigal, I was encouraged, taught, and inspired. *Praying for the Prodigal* reenergized me to have hope and trust in God, and the prayers and Scriptures were so helpful. There is much in the Bible about the prodigal, and Andrea has found those truths. The parenting ideas she gives can prevent someone from ending up with a prodigal. Therefore, this book is a double-edged sword of God's power, prevention, and solution. I applaud this author's willingness to share honestly about the struggles that contributed to the problem and then give practical instruction to help the rest of us. I know this book will bless and empower many. I highly recommend it.

~ **Kathy Collard Miller**
Speaker and best-selling author of forty-nine books,
including *Partly Cloudy with Scattered Worries*

Prodigals don't always go through outward, raging rebellion; some internalize their rebellion and reject the faith they were raised in. Andrea Merrell's words will resonate with many readers: "Every mistake I had ever made replayed in my mind like a spinning tire in a muddy rut ... I was certain God blamed me ... But there was nothing more to do except cry and pray ... and wait." *Praying for the Prodigal* will comfort hurting parents and provide assurance that God's promises are there to be claimed for the prodigal.

~ **Vie Herlocker**
Multi-published author and freelance editor,
Cornerstone-Ink.com

From cars flipping over, to late night phone calls warning her daughter would be found in a dumpster, Andrea Merrell, the mother of two ex-prodigals, has seen it all. She and her husband watched as their son and then daughter walked away from everything sacred to experience the dark side of life. In the midst of the nightmare, she cried out to God for understanding. How did this happen? How can I love my child? What are love's boundaries? Andrea shares the lessons she learned in the midst of her personal crucible. With Scripture, wise counsel, and answers from the returned prodigals themselves, this book is a must for any parent whose child has turned away from their family, faith, and God.

~ **Carol G. Stratton**
Author of *Changing Zip Codes* and *Lake Surrender*

Parents of prodigals will find hope and encouragement in Andrea Merrell's honest retelling of her family's experience with TWO prodigal children. As Andrea said, "God does not play favorites." If He did a complete restoration and redemption in answer to her prayers, He (God) is more than able to do so for others.

~ **Diana Flegal**
Agent with Hartline Literary Agency

Impacting. Touching. Heartfelt. This story of a mother's walk and wait with two prodigal children brings home the importance of what prayer, unconditional love, and faithfulness can do. Andrea Merrell writes a poignant story of her family's journey with children who are lost, then found.

~ **Cindy Sproles**
Author of *Mercy's Rain* and *New Sheets*

Dedication

Dedicated to every parent,
grandparent, and guardian who has faced
the heartache and pain of waiting for a prodigal
to return …
and especially to my wonderful family.

Acknowledgements

Writing a list of acknowledgements is a bit scary because you always think you will forget to express your appreciation to someone important. Over the years, many people—too many to count or name—have encouraged me to write down the words I have shared with them concerning their own prodigal. I say thank you to each and every one who has assured me I have something important to say; you have given me the courage to do so.

To Charlie, my husband and best friend for over forty years, *thank you* seems very inadequate. Without your constant encouragement, support, and willingness to let me sit for hours upon hours at the computer uninterrupted, I would not be able to fulfill my passion and purpose as a writer and editor. You are a true gift from heaven and the love of my life.

Thank you to my children, Jason and Rebecca, for giving me permission to be transparent and share our story. I am so very proud of both of you and love you with all my heart.

A special thanks to Billy and Dawn Claudio. You played a huge role in our story.

To Eddie Jones of Lighthouse Publishing of the Carolinas, I say thank you for helping me so much in my career—as both a writer and editor—and for giving me the opportunity to speak encouragement and hope to those who are dealing with a prodigal.

No book would be complete without the input and keen eyes of editors and beta readers. Thank you to my excellent editor, Amberlyn Dwinnell, for helping me polish my words and organize my thoughts. Thank you to Cindy Sproles for all your helpful advice and to all my wonderful beta readers for catching things the rest of us missed.

And thank you most of all to my heavenly Father who brought my family through the fire and created a story of redemption and restoration to share with others. May this book glorify His name and proclaim His faithfulness and power.

Table of Contents

For this son of mine was dead, but now he is alive;
he was lost, but now he has been found.
Luke 15:24 TEV

Introduction

As the parent or guardian of a prodigal, you've most likely experienced many sleepless nights and shed more tears than you can count. Maybe you're not the parent, but have a family member or close friend with a rebellious child causing chaos in the family.

Some of you may have small children and wonder how you can prevent them from taking the wrong path. Can this be done?

If you're searching for help and encouragement, I invite you to join me as I share the story of my prodigals, and how God protected them, restored them, and brought them back from the very flames of death and hell.

Praying for the Prodigal will strengthen your faith and help you learn to trust God completely with the life of your child/children. This book will encourage you to hold tightly to His promises and remind you to never, never give up—no matter how hopeless the situation may seem. Encouragement, Scriptures, prayers—and even practical advice from the prodigals themselves—will empower you for the battle ahead. You will also find tools to build a healthy foundation for all your children when they're young, which will equip them for the pressures they will face in this broken world.

My friend, if your child has already taken that step into a life of sin, may God hold you close as you walk through this dark valley and allow you to see His glorious light on the other side. May He grant you peace, wisdom, and the courage to do spiritual warfare for the soul of your prodigal.

From one who's been there and survived …
Andrea

CHAPTER 1

My Story – Part One

Idon't know how or when the conversation shifted. One minute we were talking about her new book … the next, her prodigal son. With tears of anguish, her story unfolded and my heart broke a little more with each word. This encounter gave me the opportunity to share my own five-year journey dealing with not one, but two prodigals, and how God not only carried us through the crisis, but brought each of us to a place of redemption and restoration.

It never fails. Everywhere I go, I meet someone dealing with a rebellious child. Because I've been there—and survived—it's easy to connect with the pain.

Webster's Collegiate Dictionary describes a prodigal as someone who is: *reckless and wasteful; someone who squanders; one who returns after an absence.* My children were teenagers when they took the wrong path, but a prodigal can be a pre-teen, a forty-year-old adult, or anywhere in between. When these individuals turn away from parental values and biblical teaching, their lives become a wasteland. They lose their potential, their health, and their destiny—sometimes even their life.

"What can I do? Is there hope for my family?" you might ask. The purpose of this book is to let you know there is *always* hope. Whenever I share my testimony, it brings great joy to see a glimmer of faith return to those who are hurting. God is not partial and never plays favorites. He is a loving Father who has given us one blessing and promise after another in His Word.

Are you or someone you love dealing with a prodigal? Maybe you're searching for ways to equip your smaller children to face future temptations. Whatever your situation, please allow my story of God's amazing grace and love—told with the permission of my former prodigals—to inspire you to believe that if He did it for me, He can do the same for you.

The Phone Call

Every muscle in my body tensed as the phone rang late one evening. I didn't know how much more bad news I could take. Was it one of my children? Another prank call? Maybe this time it was the police, the hospital, or—worse yet—the morgue.

I eased the phone to my ear and heard a raspy female voice. "I know where your daughter is and she almost OD'd."

I gasped and squeezed the receiver. My eyes closed in a feeble attempt to shut out the words and images bouncing around in my mind. My daughter—and her dad's truck— had been *missing* for days.

"Who is this?" I barely recognized my own voice.

"That's not important. Do you wanna know where she is or not? She's okay now, but yesterday her buddies said if she died, they'd throw her in a dumpster and not think another thing about it."

My hands shook and I stared at the phone in disbelief. I couldn't breathe. Tears rolled down my cheeks and my knees buckled as I slid to the floor. This was the phone call I had been dreading. Now what?

I don't remember much about the rest of the conversation, other than getting a cell phone number. All I could see was a vivid image of my baby girl lying facedown in a filthy dumpster, the life sucked out of her by God-only-knows-what—or whom. Even though the voice on the other end of the phone was unfamiliar to me, for some reason, she was willing to help. Maybe it was out of spite. I don't know what was in it for her, but regardless of the motive, God used her to throw me the first crumb of hope. My child was alive and now I knew how to contact her and bring her home.

This phone call came after several years of tears, anger, frustration, sleepless nights, and dealing with the harsh reality that both my son and daughter were caught in a lifestyle of drugs and alcohol.

They had become part of the *rough* crowd. How did things ever get to this point? I've asked myself that question hundreds of times, with no definitive answers, but let's go back to the beginning.

The Early Years

My son, three years older than my daughter, was the first to dive headlong into this rebellious lifestyle. No parent is ever fully prepared for this kind of family drama, and it was the last thing my husband Charlie and I expected. We were mortified.

Jason was not a perfect child, but he was always happy, obedient (for the most part), and well-adjusted. His constant grin earned him the nickname Smiley. Not one to be picked on, his boldness and tendency to fight back and defend himself earned him the name Tank.

The preschool years had many ups and downs, but Charlie and I were having fun as new parents with our dark-haired, dark-eyed, adorable baby boy. When we felt like something was missing, we prayed for a little girl to make our family complete.

Jason was three when our daughter was born, and he was excited about her arrival. But as Rebecca got older and began to invade his territory, Jason, like most other kids, realized he was no longer the key player in the home. He now had to share his toys, along with the attention of his parents. Our family dynamic changed as sibling rivalry became an issue. It was an ongoing problem for all of us.

In spite of the conflicts, as Rebecca got older she adored her big brother. We watched our blond-haired, blue-eyed princess follow Jason around, longing for his attention. We knew he loved her, but he constantly chose to either pick on or ignore her. This only made her go to greater lengths to get his attention—something he didn't handle very well. It was a challenge for him and something he would deal with for years to come.

School brought our son a whole new set of challenges.

One thing my husband and I wish we had realized early-on was the importance of preparing our children as much as possible for things they would face in a school setting. This is becoming an even more critical issue as our society deteriorates. Peer pressure and bullying have escalated. Secular humanism is taught, and violence erupts in schools all over the country. Kids as young as seven and eight are being lured into taking drugs and getting involved in all sorts of sexual activities—even pornography.

A number of factors enter in—personality, basic temperament, likes, dislikes, abilities, background, passions—but there is much wisdom we can impart to help children through the rough times. The most important responsibility is teaching them the Word of God and how to depend on Him when things are beyond their control.

Looking back, I can see how ill-prepared my son was for this new phase of life.

Elementary school started off well enough, even though Jason was younger than most of the other kids in his class. He attended a private Christian school in Florida and was blessed with patient and caring teachers. When we moved to South Carolina and he entered the third grade in the public school system, his teacher had little tolerance for … well, just about anything. She brought out the worst in our son in every way.

That year, we noticed a subtle change in Jason's behavior and the way he dealt with things. His grades dropped and he struggled with classwork. His teacher complained about his behavior, attention span, and the fact that most of the other students were three to six months older. She would have been happy to stick him back in the second grade or put him in a *slow* class, but we wouldn't allow it. As far as we were concerned, this was all part of growing up and being in a new school.

Looking back, we know moving Jason out of this teacher's class would have been the best thing for him, even if it meant repeating the third grade. We also realize we should have been more involved in our child's education.

Homeschooling was not an option for us at that time, but more and more parents are leaning toward the homeschool process. If that's the process you choose, use that time to equip your child mentally, emotionally, and spiritually, but don't forget to prepare them for stepping out into the world. If your child is in public school, keep your eyes, ears, and heart fine-tuned to what's going on there. Know the teachers and know your child's friends. Don't smother or be overprotective, but show interest and be a safe place for your child to come when he has questions or problems. If there is a person or situation negatively affecting your family, don't ignore it. We ignored some important signs, and it cost us dearly in many ways.

Jason's middle-school years passed without incident. He and his sister still didn't get along well, and he was not crazy about school, but both were involved in church and youth activities. There were times, however—even in Christian environments—when our kids didn't feel accepted or as *good* as the other kids. Pressure to measure up to a certain standard caused their self-esteem to waver. They started saying and doing things to get the attention and affirmation they so desperately needed. Because Charlie and I consider ourselves loyal to a fault, we have stayed in the wrong environment on several occasions much longer than we should have. Unfortunately, our children were the ones who suffered the most.

A word of warning: Don't think all people who profess to be Christians will automatically treat you or your children in a Christ-like manner. It hurts me to say that sometimes the *unsaved* will treat us with more respect than fellow believers. It's been said that Christians are the first to "shoot their wounded," and we've found much truth in that statement over the years. If you find yourself in an unhealthy environment with red flags popping up all around, it may be time to abandon ship.

We can now see many scenarios that adversely affected our family. If we had been truly listening to our children—more aware of the pressure they were under and its damaging effects—we would have done things very differently. Too bad there are no do-overs.

All things considered, we kept doing the best we knew how, still believing our family was *okay*. Once Jason reached high school, we thought we were in the home stretch. Never big on sports, our son was a typical computer nerd. He loved electronics and any type of gadget. He enjoyed reading and could do most anything he set his mind to. Jason was not a big talker; he was a thinker and a bit of a loner.

He was, in our estimation, a good kid.

Our First Prodigal Leaves Home

In Jason's senior year, everything changed. I watched my tall, handsome son withdraw from his family and everything *good* in his life. He rarely attended church or church activities, and we stopped eating meals as a family. The easy-going nature, brilliant smile, and twinkle in his eyes we had always loved … disappeared. He became sullen and hard to get along with, especially after graduation. His late nights and unwholesome activities made it almost impossible for him to get up in the mornings. Many times he didn't. He lost jobs, friends, and the respect of all the people who loved and cared about him, and it didn't seem to bother him in the least.

Our son was showing classic signs of drug and alcohol abuse, but at the time, we were unaware and didn't know how to deal with him. We later realized how crucial it is for parents to not only teach their children the dangers of substance abuse, but to educate themselves on how to recognize the signs. No child or parent is immune. Unfortunately, this can happen to anyone.

Teens are caught between childhood and adulthood. This is a confusing place for them, even in the best-case scenario. Emotions, hormones, and thought processes are like a giant yo-yo, and kids are constantly trying to find out where they fit. They need someone who understands.

The truth is that teens have stress, just like the rest of us. If we downplay the things they face because we don't think their problems are big enough to worry about, they will resent us. We say, "Grow up and act your age." Well, they would if they knew how. When they try to act like an adult, we say, "No way, you're just a kid." Thus, we add to the confusion and frustration they're already dealing with. Unless we find a way to love and support them through this transition, they will find someone—or some*thing*—to make them feel better about themselves. This gives them a false sense of control.

Because Charlie and I didn't understand these concepts, we failed in so many different ways. To keep Jason from losing his car, we made payments as long as we could. But when we couldn't keep up with the extra expense, he lost it anyway. We learned a hard lesson: children need to be responsible for their own actions. We also found out the "tough love" principle is actually tougher on the parent than the child.

Things only worsened and our son became a virtual stranger living in our home. He was disrespectful, irresponsible, and took advantage of us at every turn. Charlie and I were clueless. We had no friends or family members who had ever faced this situation and, frankly, we didn't want the whole world to know what was going on. We felt like total failures.

Our Daughter Becomes a Prodigal

We tried to hold our family together, but it wasn't long before Rebecca, who still idolized her brother, followed him down this dark path. She had finally found a connection with him, even though it was sinful, illegal, and dangerous.

Jason's attitude toward her changed and they started getting along and having fun for the first time. She was still in high school, but as long as they were partying together, their relationship blossomed.

Having a rebellious son was hard enough, but watching our beautiful daughter march boldly into a life of destruction was heart-wrenching. I've often wondered how the story of the prodigal son (see Luke 15) would have turned out if the older brother had left too—how the father's heart would have broken to lose both his children to an ungodly lifestyle.

From the time she was conceived, Rebecca was special. Charlie and I longed for a daughter, and God gave us the desire of our hearts. She brought such joy to our family and grew into a loving, caring individual with tremendous potential. She enjoyed learning about everything, being with people, and gave 100 percent to whatever she tackled. She was a leader, but also very influenced by peer pressure. During the high school years, we watched her pull away, just as Jason had done.

Rebecca's love of school, sports, and family dwindled to nothing. After graduation, her choice of friends caused us great concern. She lost her scholarship to a local university because she couldn't concentrate, be on time, or get along with her professors. She became more and more distant. It got to the point that we never knew where she was, who she was with, and when or *if* she was coming home. When she *was* at home, there were arguments and far too many harsh, hateful words—from all of us.

The nights were long and my pillow permanently tear-stained. I felt old and tired as stress took a huge toll on me. Charlie tried to be strong for both of us, but I could see the effect it had on him. He had always been so proud of his children. We both had.

But we now found ourselves in a battle for our family and the souls of our children.

During this terrible season in our lives, reckless driving and car accidents made our insurance so high we could barely afford it. There were many trips to the hospital with both kids. I vividly remember one such incident.

Charlie and I were on our way home from church when we got a call from one of Jason and Rebecca's friends.

"Jason had an accident. He flipped the car at the end of your road. Rebecca's hurt bad and you need to hurry."

The line went dead.

I choked back tears and the lump in my throat as I repeated the phone call to Charlie. He didn't say a word, just stepped on the gas and raced down the highway. Thankfully, we were only a few minutes from home. My husband's knuckles were white as he gripped the steering wheel, and I tried to stay calm. I couldn't think ... didn't know what to say. I closed my eyes, leaned my head against the cold glass and kept repeating, "Jesus, Jesus, Jesus," until Charlie screeched to a stop a few feet from the overturned SUV.

My hands flew to my face as I took in the scene, but my kids were nowhere in sight. Charlie and I both jumped from the car and rushed toward the wreckage. A patrolman ran toward us and asked if we were the parents. His next words slammed into me with brute force.

"I'm sorry. Your son seems to be okay, but your daughter is seriously hurt. She's been airlifted to Memorial Hospital."

"Airlifted? Why? What's wrong?" my husband barked at the patrolman.

"Yes sir. When the car flipped over, the windows were down and your daughter's hand was caught underneath, between the car and the pavement. EMS didn't want to take a chance on her losing that hand."

I grabbed Charlie's arm as my legs started to buckle. His face was deathly pale. We held on to each other as we rushed back to the car.

The patrolman called after us, "By the way, there was another young woman in the car."

We reached the hospital in record time, probably breaking every traffic law, while begging God the entire time to have mercy on our children. When we got to the emergency room, we had no idea what we might face. As it turned out, both of our kids were fine, but my son's girlfriend was in surgery.

We learned that Jason, who never wore his seatbelt, happened to have it on this time. When the car flipped, he was hanging upside down, strapped in the seatbelt which saved his life. He quickly got out of the car and—with an adrenaline rush and the help of his friend who made the phone call—lifted the car enough for his girlfriend to free her hand. She was the one airlifted to the hospital while my children rode in an ambulance.

I later found out from a friend at church that she had seen the helicopter as it landed at the hospital. She'd spent time praying for the person who was injured. That could be the very reason the hand was saved.

The young man who called us climbed out of the car, made his call, and disappeared. He had his own issues with the police and didn't want to get caught.

God spared my children from what could have been certain death. His mercies were truly amazing that day.

Over the years, we spent far too much time in the magistrate's office as a result of reckless behavior and poor choices. One day, years after the fact, our daughter told us about a wild party she attended. Her foolishness caused her to fall backwards off a deck at least fifteen feet, but she was unscathed.

Time after time, God protected our children when we had no clue what was going on.

Expenses escalated. Tickets, insurance, and hospital bills were outrageous. Neither of our children could hold on to a job to help support themselves, so everything defaulted back to us.

The blatant disrespect for us and for God was a burden we felt unable to carry. My husband and I faced this situation day-in and day-out, with no end in sight. It was one of the darkest times of my life, and I struggled to trust God and believe His promises. As one day morphed into another, things only grew worse.

If this is where you are, know that you are not alone. I have been there—others have been there—and we've all felt the agonizing pain and sense of loss and utter despair. Many of us have also seen God move mightily in our situation, so don't give up hope.

The Blame Game

If you're dealing with a prodigal, you know the blame game all too well. If you're like me, you think *you* are the one at fault, and you carry a tremendous load of guilt and condemnation. I blamed myself for everything, beating myself up mentally on a regular basis. I told God it was surely all my fault and questioned why He ever allowed me to become a parent in the first place, especially if He knew I wasn't capable of handling the responsibility. Every mistake I had ever made replayed in my mind like a spinning tire in a muddy rut.

Maybe you believe you did everything you should have done and can't figure out where you went wrong. That was one of my biggest struggles. Charlie and I did all the *right* things. We took our children to church, prayed with (and for) them daily, and raised them in a godly environment. They went to Sunday school, VBS, and Christian camps. They never listened to secular music or read secular books. They could quote Scripture verses and knew all the words to the most popular Christian songs. Born again and baptized at a very early age, they were good, upstanding, obedient kids. What could have possibly gone wrong?

The staggering truth is: Even *good* kids rebel—and even *good* parents can end up with a prodigal. Don't let anyone put you on a guilt trip.

Statistics say, "88 percent of children raised in an evangelical Christian home will leave the church by the age of eighteen." According to a 2011 Barna survey, "Three out of four young people leave the faith these days. But the good news for worried parents is that about half of those kids will find their way back."

Those are staggering statistics. I just never thought it would happen to my family. Yet, here I was, crying myself to sleep at night, cringing with fear every time the phone rang. My son and daughter were running from everything they had been taught—everything their father and I had tried to model before them and instill in their hearts. Fear of the unknown—of the future—became the norm, and it was suffocating the life out of both of us.

It's difficult enough to have one child take the wrong path, but two at the same time brings double the amount of guilt, fear, and frustration. Raising teenagers is never easy, but when you go to bed at night and wonder when and *if* your children are going to come home, it's agonizing. It raises the stakes and brings parents to their knees.

I cried out on a regular basis, *God, how can this be happening? What more could we have done? Where are you?*

God didn't seem to be listening. Didn't He care?

Is that how you are feeling? Are you ready to give up?

It would be impossible to count the number of times I wanted to give up.

I'm over it, God. They can do whatever they want to. If they're determined to go to hell, I can't stop them. I can't live like this. I'm not praying anymore!

That would last for about thirty seconds, and then my earnest prayers and tears would begin again. I knew God loved my children even more than I did, and He would take care of them, but my mother's heart was shattered and I wanted my family back.

I know that's the cry of your heart too.

Only a few people knew about our situation, and they kept telling us not to worry. They assured us our children were raised in *the nurture and admonition of the Lord* (see Ephesians 6:4 KJV) and He would turn things around. "You've put the Word of God in them and you have to believe it will produce fruit." We heard this continually, but it was hard to receive.

Easy for them to say; they've never been through anything like this, was my first thought.

If people are telling you not to worry and that everything will be okay, remember they mean well. When others haven't walked in your shoes—haven't lived with the agony you experience day in and day out—they don't always know what to say.

The things Charlie and I endured during this time were painful—cruel—heartbreaking. To use the expression, "Been there—done that—got the T-shirt," I can say I have a whole closet full. The strain and stress of living in this dysfunctional mess was overwhelming.

I begged my husband to pack up my children's things and put them out of the house permanently, once and for all, but he refused. He never had peace about doing something that drastic and, deep down, neither did I. It just seemed like it would be easier to deal with if it wasn't constantly in my face. I kept looking for that bright light at the end of the proverbial tunnel, but all was total darkness.

I need a sign, God—something to hold on to. Please show me what to do.

This type of prayer became my daily routine as I looked for a change—any change—and saw none. I was certain God blamed me for bad parenting and had turned His back on our family. But there was nothing more to do except cry and pray.

And wait.

CHAPTER 2

My Story – Part Two

After five long years of agony—what seemed an entire lifetime—the first answer to my prayers finally came at a Wednesday night church service. At the end of the service, my pastor took the microphone from our visiting speaker and said words that grabbed my heart like a vise.

"I can't get away from this. I believe there's a parent here who is agonizing over a prodigal child, and the Lord wants to minister to you." His eyes swept the congregation and he waited. The compassion on his face was my undoing.

I stood up and stepped forward, not missing the surprised look on his face. After all, I had been the church secretary for years and he was not aware of the gravity of the situation. Charlie and I had never confided in him or asked for help. Maybe it was embarrassment, maybe pride, but whatever the reason, trying to carry the burden alone was unhealthy and unscriptural.

The visiting speaker didn't know me or anything about my family. My pastor prayed, and then the speaker's wife walked over, wrapped her arms around me, and began to pray in earnest. We both cried. I trembled from head to toe. I don't remember a single word she said, but I do remember how I felt.

Something happened on the inside that I can't explain. I felt a release in my spirit. A tremendous weight lifted off my shoulders. For the first time since my nightmare began, I was able to lay my burden at the foot of the cross and leave it there. I knew, without a doubt, God had not only heard my prayers, but He was working all things together for my good and the good of my children (see Romans 8:28).

A spark of hope was rekindled.

The Biggest Change Was in Me

Even though I knew something had shifted, there was no instantaneous miracle—at least not one that could be seen. My children didn't come home that night, the next, or the next. The biggest change took place in *me* as God wrapped His arms around me and drew me closer than I'd ever been before. As I confessed my fears and failures, He washed me clean and renewed my mind. I knew I was forgiven. The guilt and condemnation fell away, and God replaced them with assurance and a new sense of freedom.

Consumed with negative thoughts and worry about my children—convinced I was the problem in the first place—I had gradually let my relationship with the Lord slip. By refusing to pray for myself or let Him work in me, I had missed the blessing of His comfort and guidance.

Now, for the first time in years, I was able to petition God and stand upon His Word with boldness and confidence. My peace and joy returned, and each time I lifted my son and daughter up in prayer, God would prompt me to pray in different ways, all according to His Word. I had been praying daily for my children for years, but now the prayers were different. They carried a power they never had before. I found myself doing spiritual warfare, renouncing the enemy and the spirits of darkness harassing my children. I bound the spirits of conquest, control, and addiction over them.

One day, as I was driving to work, praying for Jason and Rebecca, God impressed me to speak directly to their spirits, their innermost being, stirring the life of God on the inside. I'd never done this before and it seemed strange, but I obeyed. I claimed them for the kingdom of God and told the enemy he would not have them any longer. God was orchestrating my prayers and assuring me He would save my children and bring them home—not only to their earthly parents, but to their heavenly Father who was also waiting for them to return.

My husband and I had finally been thrown a lifeline.

The weeks went by and nothing appeared to change in the natural realm, but there was a definite change in the spiritual realm. Charlie was confident, and my heart settled for the first time. We both knew we would continue to love our kids unconditionally, pray for them, and do whatever we had to do to win them back—no matter how long it took.

The Breakthrough

Our breakthrough came a couple of months after the Wednesday night service. Jason started hanging around the house more than he had in the five years we had watched him and his sister walk down the wrong path. It was obvious he had something on his mind, but was hesitant to approach us. One day, he told his dad how miserable he was. He talked about how he would separate himself from the crowd and find a place to be alone, crying and asking how he had ever gotten his life in such a mess. He was under conviction and looking for a way out. We were ready to help him find it.

With strength only God can give, Jason made a choice. He turned his back on the life he had been living, surrendered himself completely to God, distanced himself from his unsavory friends, and was supernaturally delivered from drugs and alcohol—without the first sign of withdrawal. We found out later that Jason had not only taken drugs, he had also sold them. Many of his friends were caught and some served time, but God showed Himself strong and mighty on behalf of our son.

A miracle.

Our hope was renewed. Charlie and I knew deep in our hearts it was only a matter of time before our daughter would follow, especially once she found out her brother was back on the right path. Their partying days were over.

It only took a few weeks.

The night we received the phone call about my daughter was when everything changed. Rebecca and one of her friends had *borrowed* her dad's truck without permission. Now that we had a phone number, Charlie—not knowing what else to do—called and left a stern message:

"If you're not home by tomorrow with my truck parked in the driveway, I'll call the police and report it stolen." This was her wake-up call.

When Rebecca returned home the next day, we all knew she had hit bottom—hard.

Because she was easily swayed by the people around her, we knew it was imperative to send her away from all the ungodly influences in her life. We looked into Teen Challenge and a number of other options, but Charlie suggested contacting her former youth pastors, Billy and Dawn Claudio. I made the phone call, presented our dilemma to Billy, and asked if there was any possibility we could send our daughter to their home for a short time.

I will never forget the answer.

Without hesitation … without saying, "I'll pray about it" … without saying, "I'll talk to Dawn about it," he said this one incredible word—"Absolutely!"

Another miracle.

Three days later, I put Rebecca on a plane to Arizona. My daughter was literally skin and bones, her face pasty white, her eyes dark and lifeless. She looked like *walking death*. My heart twisted as she stepped away to board the plane, but God whispered His assurance, letting me know she was in His hands.

The weeks passed slowly, but we continued to pray. We only heard from Rebecca a couple of times, mumbling about how hard this was for her. I thought about the Scripture in Proverbs that talks about correcting our children while there's hope, in spite of their crying—or in this case, in spite of whining and complaining (see Proverbs 19:18). This was like a trip to the doctor for stitches; it was painful for the moment, but necessary for healing.

We had renewed faith our daughter would be completely restored.

Seven weeks later I flew to Arizona to pick her up, not knowing what to expect. Rebecca had begun the journey back to the Lord, but we were certain there would still be a lot of work to do when we got her back home.

I could not have been more surprised—or wrong.

The young woman who met me at the airport looked nothing like the one I had sent away. She had gained some much-needed weight, her skin was glowing, and her eyes radiated with the love and the life of Christ. She was truly transformed from the inside/out. Our sweet, beautiful, bright-eyed girl was back. We clung to each other, laughing and crying for what seemed like hours. For the next few days, I marveled at the *new* Rebecca. I couldn't take my eyes off of her, nor could I stop thanking God for what He had done in her heart.

Truly, another miracle.

I don't know exactly what took place in those seven weeks, other than discipline, hard work, prayer, and Bible study—coupled with lots of love and encouragement by two very special people who were willing to disrupt their normal routine, take in a rebellious teenager, and be used mightily by the Lord. I do know with certainty it was a divine appointment for our daughter. We like to refer to her time in Scottsdale as spiritual boot camp.

Today

That was over thirteen years ago. Today, my son is married to a beautiful Christian woman and has three delightful little girls. He has worked in both children's ministry and student ministry at church. A few years ago, I listened as he gave his testimony to the students at summer camp. My heart swelled with pride and my eyes filled with tears as I thought about how far God has brought him. Knowing that many of his friends spent time in jail or are still living a reckless lifestyle, I am reminded how thankful I am for God's faithfulness to His children.

My daughter is now the mother of two precious little girls. She is married to a man who loves, serves, and honors God in every way. She is a hard-working mom with a tender, giving spirit. She loves the Lord with all her heart and has a desire to help others who have gone through the things she has faced and conquered. I now have a friend as well as a daughter. Her life could have been snuffed out prematurely that horrible day we got the phone call. If she had ended up in a dumpster, we may never have known what happened to her.

But God had other plans.

Through prayer, God brought my prodigals home. He also brought me back to a place of faith and confidence that was swept away by fear and worry. We all experienced true redemption and restoration.

My children are living proof that God is faithful, true to His Word, and ready to work miracles in the lives of those who will dare to believe Him.

What about you? Will you dare to believe? Let's take a look at your story and discover how you can pray for your prodigal, while building a strong and healthy foundation to keep your younger children on the right path.

CHAPTER 3

Your Story – What Can You Do?

If you're in the middle of a crisis with your child, my heart breaks for you. Because I've faced the agony and lived through the turmoil, I can relate to your questions and fear.

But I'm here to tell you there is hope.

They say it's darkest just before dawn—the moment that first ray of light breaks through the night and dispels the darkness. You never know when your answer is just over the horizon. If I learned anything through those dark days, it is that God is loving and faithful, His Word is true, and prayer works. The most important lesson was this: No matter how impossible the situation seems, never give up and never stop praying.

So, what's your story? Even though the details are different from mine, the pain is the same. We all love our children and want the best for them. Most parents think, "That could never happen to my family."

That's what I thought—but I was wrong.

Am I saying I did everything right? Absolutely not. There were many moments of anger and ungodly outbursts. There were times I judged and criticized instead of loving and nurturing. My husband and I tried to practice tough love, but it was much tougher than we ever imagined. The Bible tells us not to provoke our children, causing anger and hurt, and there were countless times we both failed miserably in that department.

Do I have all the answers? Again, absolutely not. But in order for God to turn things around and work them for our good and His glory, we must share our experiences and victories with others. Nothing is wasted in God's economy and He expects us to pay it forward. Whatever we face in this life can be effectively used as a tool to help someone else. Whatever the enemy means for evil and destruction, God can counteract and turn into a blessing.

Hopefully, my story and the lessons God taught me will help bring you and your family to a place of restoration and peace.

First Steps

Listed below are four keys that will make all the difference in fighting this battle and emerging victorious, no matter where you are in your journey.

- **Trusting God:** The first key is to trust God with your whole heart—no matter what you see, hear, think, or feel. Make sure you maintain a right relationship with Him. It's easy to become bitter and resentful, even toward your own children, especially when you feel abused and betrayed. It's essential to walk in love and forgiveness. Sometimes it's harder to forgive ourselves than it is others. That was certainly true for me.

- **Prayer:** The second key is to commit your children to God and pray for them daily.

Make this your first priority and do it whether you feel like it or not. It's difficult to pray for someone when you're angry, but I assure you that as you pray, your heart will change and you'll see the situation differently—through God's eyes. Don't wait for large blocks of time when you can read, study, and pray. Talk to God about your child all through the day—and even throughout the night. His ear is always attentive to our needs.

- **Unconditional Love:** Love your children unconditionally. It doesn't matter whether they sell drugs, go to jail, or even commit murder. Sin is sin, but our children need to know we love them—regardless—and we will never turn our backs on them. It's essential to let them know we don't condone their actions, but neither do we condemn them as a person. That's not our job. If we judge and condemn, we will *be* judged and condemned—a hard concept, but a scriptural one.

- **Accountability:** Know that you are not responsible for their decisions. Yes, parenting is important, but—ultimately—people make their own choices. Allow your children to be responsible for their own actions. Don't be so quick to bail them out, like we did by paying Jason's car payment. Sometimes children have to suffer the consequences of their actions and learn the hard way—just like we do—especially if they refuse to listen. Sometimes the harder the lesson, the better it *sticks*. Keep them accountable.

One thing to remember is that our children do not *belong* to us. They belong to God. We are only their earthly guardians—caretakers—examples. We must be wise stewards with whatever God places in our care, even when the task is challenging.

Boundaries

One of my biggest regrets is not establishing a healthy foundation and creating reasonable boundaries when my children were small. When we take the time and effort to put these guidelines in place, it's easier to recognize the conflicting signals as our children hold tightly to us with one hand and push us away with the other. This means they're struggling for independence—which is good because that's exactly how God designed them. Just like the baby bird cannot stay in the nest forever, our children must learn to fly. Our job is to let them go, but assure them they have a soft place to *land* when they fall.

My greatest challenge as a parent has been the ability to be firm without becoming angry. This is why boundaries are so important—no matter what age your children happen to be. Make reasonable rules everyone can live with, and be sure to enforce them when they're broken. Children and teenagers will test the limits continually, and they are counting on us to be consistent. They *want* guidelines and parameters, whether they realize it or not. It makes them feel loved, secure, and safe.

Be open, honest, and transparent with your children. They can see through pretense. Be quick to apologize when you mess up, no matter how many times it happens. Pride and arrogance will drive a wedge between you and your children. Admit the fact that you're not perfect and you don't have all the answers—they already know. They will respect your honesty and humility, whether they show it or not. This will accelerate the healing process down the road. Believe me ... there will come a day when your prodigal says to you, "Thank you. Now I understand. Please forgive me for what I put you through."

Be the parent, the adult—not the cool friend. There will be plenty of time to be friends later. Children need a guide, an example, a stable, focused adult to give them direction. It's vital to maintain your character and integrity by not compromising and lowering your standards.

Stay Firm and Calm

Love acts; it does not react. Sometimes our children will push all the right buttons to get a reaction. Resist the urge to give in. It's not easy, but practice self-control. Don't allow yourself to be bullied or intimidated by a rebellious teenager, or even a thirty-year-old. Keeping a cool head in the midst of chaos speaks much louder than allowing kids to gain the upper hand by bringing us down to their level. When we stay calm, it drives them crazy ... and makes them think.

Be sure you and your spouse—or other family members if you are a single parent—are on the same page in how you deal with the situation. Children have a natural tendency to play one authority figure against another. When this happens, no one wins.

If you need help, seek godly counsel. Find a support group. If one is not available, create one. Many other parents/guardians would benefit from this type of support.

Don't Stop Praying

Whatever you do, please don't stop praying. During the times my son was alone and questioning how he had gotten his life in such a mess, it's very likely those were times his dad and I were on our knees pleading for God's mercy and grace. Jason told us the harder he tried to run, the more he was drawn back to his roots. It was impossible for him to get away from his foundation—or from God.

When my daughter was rescued from death on more than one occasion, God was listening to the prayers of grieving parents, dispatching His angels, and performing His Word on everyone's behalf. Numbers 23:19 (NIV) says, *God is not a man, that he should lie, nor a son of man, that he should change his mind. Does he speak and then not act? Does he promise and not fulfill?* In Ezekiel 12:25, The Message translation states, *I, God, am doing the speaking. What I say happens. None of what I say is on hold. What I say, I'll do . . .*

What if we had stopped praying? If we had not taken God's Word literally as our only truth and salvation, our story may not have had a happy ending.

Every child is different ... every story unique. Don't compare your circumstances with others. God rarely moves the same from one situation to the next, but one thing is certain: One single word from God can change the entire course of someone's life. He knows your prodigal better than you do, and He knows how to reach him.

Be careful not to put limitations on God or expect Him to move on your time frame. Even though God's methods and timetable are different from ours, He has promised to answer when we come to Him and ask in faith, believing He will do what He said He would do. His Spirit will give you specific promises to stand on. When He does, stand firm and don't let yourself be shaken by the darkness and the lies of the enemy.

And don't be afraid to vent. Be real with God. Tell Him how you feel. He already knows and will never shun or condemn you for your honesty.

The most important thing you can do is pray like your life—and the life of your prodigal—depends upon it. It does!

A Parent's Checklist for Survival

Here is a recap of what we've talked about so far. Read over these survival tips as often as you need to. Post them somewhere you can see them every day. Add to the list as God speaks to your heart. It's important to know you're not alone, which is one of Satan's biggest lies. Remember that others have walked this rocky path before you and have emerged victorious.

- ✓ Trust God with your whole heart and keep your eyes on Him—not your problem.

- ✓ Believe with every fiber of your being that His promises are true—and they are for *you*.

- ✓ Cast your care on Him. Lay this burden at His feet and leave it there.

- ✓ Commit your children to God.

- ✓ Pray for them daily without fail.

- ✓ Love your children unconditionally.

- ✓ Forgive your children.

- ✓ Forgive yourself.

- ✓ Don't judge or condemn—your children or yourself.

- ✓ Listen closely to your children and make time for them.

- ✓ Respect their feelings.

✓ Practice tough love. Hold your children accountable for their actions.

✓ Be the parent—not the cool friend.

✓ Don't compromise or lower your standards.

✓ Practice self-control. Learn to act—not react.

✓ Learn the early signs of drug and alcohol abuse—and what to do about it.

✓ Set boundaries and take charge, but be flexible.

✓ Don't let your children *demand* privileges.

✓ Find Scriptures that speak specifically and directly to you. Confess them daily.

✓ Don't be afraid to vent to God. Tell Him how you feel. He already knows.

✓ Seek godly counsel. Don't try to carry this by yourself.

✓ Don't take bad behavior personally or become angry, bitter, and resentful.

✓ Don't get caught in the blame game.

✓ Let the peace of God rule in your heart and allow His joy to be your strength.

✓ No matter how tempting it might be— never give up on your children.

CHAPTER 4

Your Hope – Prayers for Your Prodigal

Your hope must be in God and God alone. Your only weapon against the attacks of the enemy, Satan, is the powerful, life-giving Word of God—the sword of the spirit. Jesus defeated the enemy in the wilderness by saying repeatedly, *It is written* (see Matthew chapter 4 NIV). How can we expect to defeat him any other way?

Satan is a thief. He's out to steal your children and their destiny. It's your job as a godly parent/guardian to protect your children with love, encouragement, and—most of all—prayer.

Use this chapter to fill your arsenal with Scriptures that apply to your circumstances. Read them. Study them. Memorize them. Post

them where you can see them daily. Pray them
out loud. Make them personal. Insert your child's
name and be specific when naming certain sins
or situations.

Romans 10:17 (NKJV) says: *So then faith comes
by hearing, and hearing by the word of God.* There
is no greater way to build *your* faith than for *your*
ears to hear *your* own voice speaking the truth
of the Scriptures. The more you pray the Word,
the stronger your faith will grow and the more
powerful your prayers will become.

You may be plagued with the question, "But
what if they *never* come back?" My answer is,
"But what if they *do?*" Because you don't know
the future outcome for any given situation,
praying for your children is the same as praying
for finances, healing, or any other pressing
need.

The Bible tells us to ask/confess/believe in
faith. That means believing God will do what
He says He will do. Do you believe it's His will
for your children to be restored? In Luke 18:16-
17 (TEV), Jesus said, *Let the children come to me*

and do not stop them, because the kingdom of God belongs to such as these.

When you pray, do not doubt, fear, or waver. *But when he asks, he must believe and not doubt, because he who doubts is like a wave of the sea, blown and tossed by the wind. That man should not think he will receive anything from the Lord; he is a double-minded man, unstable in all he does* (James 1:6-8 NIV).

We are instructed throughout Scripture to rejoice and give thanks to God, not *for* all things, but *in* all things. Praise and thanksgiving bring God into the midst of your situation, along with assurance and peace of mind. *Rejoice in the Lord always. I will say it again: Rejoice! Let your gentleness be evident to all. The Lord is near. Do not be anxious about anything, but in everything, by prayer and petition, with thanksgiving, present your requests to God. And the peace of God, which transcends all understanding, will guard your hearts and your minds in Christ Jesus* (Philippians 4:4-7 NIV).

Remember … God loves your children even more than you do, and He knows how to reach them and turn their hearts toward Him.

Moving Out of Your Comfort Zone

When I opened my heart to the Spirit of God and looked to Him to lead me as I lifted up my children in prayer, He gave me many different ways to pray for them. He'll do the same for you. Even if it seems odd or uncomfortable to pray these promises out loud, do it anyway. Your confidence will grow and you will release faith-filled words that will never return void.

Many people are uncertain about confessing something that is not clearly evident. Don't be hesitant to call *things that are not as though they were* (see Romans 4:17 NIV). When we talk about childlike faith, we might picture a small boy asking for a treat or special toy. If a parent promises something to that boy—especially if the parent is someone who keeps their word— that boy does not have to *see* it to *believe* it. He simply takes the word of someone who loves him and wants the best for him. He can rest confidently in the fact that it will happen.

If you are in need of healing, you can boldly pray Scriptures such as Isaiah 53:5 KJV (*with His stripes we are healed*), Psalm 107:20 KJV (*He sent*

His Word, and healed them, and delivered them from their destructions), or 3 John 2 NKJV (*Beloved, I pray that you may prosper in all things and be in health, just as your soul prospers*).

To take it a step further, if you are in need of a financial blessing, you can pray the following Scriptures: Philippians 4:19 KJV (*But my God shall supply all your need according to His riches in glory by Christ Jesus*), or Luke 6:38 NIV (*Give and it will be given to you. A good measure, pressed down, shaken together and running over, will be poured into your lap*).

Keep God's Word in context. His Word is conditional and when we meet the condition, He will deliver on the promise. When His Word works *in* you, it will work *for* you.

God spoke the world into existence when there was nothing to be seen. When you thank God (in advance) that your children are obedient, respectful, and living lives pleasing to the Lord, it will sound strange at first—even radical and maybe a little foolish—but that's what faith is about. Without it, we cannot please Him. *And without faith it is impossible to please God, because anyone who comes to him must believe that he exists and that he rewards those who earnestly seek him* (Hebrews 11:6 NIV).

How do we define faith? Hebrews 11:1(AMP) says, *Now faith is the assurance (the confirmation, the title deed) of the things [we] hope for, being the proof of things [we] do not see and the conviction of their reality [faith perceiving as real fact what is not revealed to the senses].*

The Living Bible puts it this way: *What is faith? It is the confident assurance that something we want is going to happen. It is the certainty that what we hope for is waiting for us, even though we cannot see it up ahead.*

When we belong to God, He sees us through the shed blood of Jesus and the reality of His Word. We must learn to see our children through His eyes and believe He will bring these things to pass. When we trust Him, delight in Him, and commit our ways to Him, He promises to give us the desires of our heart and cause us to rest in Him. (See Psalm 37:4-7).

But What If My Prodigal is Not a Christian?

The same principles apply. Again, God knows how to reach your child, saved or unsaved. *Believe in the Lord Jesus, and you will be saved—you and your household* (Acts 16:31 NIV). Pray for salvation and deliverance.

Praying the Word of God

A commitment to daily prayer is essential. It's been said that anything you do consistently for thirty days will become a habit. When you pray His Word habitually, God will not only move in the hearts and lives of your children and show Himself strong on their behalf, He will work in you. As you learn to let go, cast your cares on Him, and allow Him to work in His time and in His way, God will bring you to a place of rest. The more you do this, the easier it will become and the more God will honor your faith. Be sure to listen for His voice and pray as He leads.

As you pray, listen for that still, small voice as God adds His words to yours. Don't be moved by situations and circumstances. Sometimes things get worse before they get better. If they do, it's not because your prayers are not effective or not being heard. This is the time to press in and be tenacious with your faith. Whenever you pray the Word of God, know that you are praying according to His perfect will.

Here's a prayer to get you started:

Father, work in _____ (insert your child's name) and in me as I commit to daily prayer. I praise You and open my heart to Your Spirit to guide me. Give me courage to stand strong and flexibility to follow Your leading. Keep hope kindled within me, and help me trust You with the life of my precious child. Fill me with peace. Your joy is my strength and it doesn't depend on my circumstances or what I see with my natural eye.

Thirty Days of Prayers for the Prodigal

Now it's your turn. Use the prayers in this section as a guideline, and let the Holy Spirit lead you. Prayers are not magical words or formulas, and God is not a genie in a lamp. He responds to a heart that is fully committed to Him and believes in the power and authority of His Word.

Jesus said in Mark 11:23 (NIV), *I tell you the truth, if anyone says to this mountain, "Go, throw yourself into the sea," and does not doubt in his heart but believes that what he says will happen, it will be done for him. Therefore I tell you, whatever you ask for in prayer, believe that you have received it, and it will be yours.*

Day One

Father, You said I can walk free of guilt and condemnation. I've made a lot of mistakes with my children, but I know their choices are not my fault. Your Word says if I confess my sins, You will forgive and cleanse me from all unrighteousness—all wrong thoughts, deeds, words, and attitudes. I ask forgiveness and receive it now in Jesus' name. Give me boldness and confidence to stand in the gap and do spiritual warfare for my children. Strengthen me for the battle ahead.

- *There is no condemnation for those who belong to Christ Jesus.* **Romans 8:1-2 NLT**
- *If we confess our sins, He is faithful and just to forgive us our sins and to cleanse us from all unrighteousness.*
  1 John 1:9 NKJV

Day Two

Lord, I have done the best I could to raise my children in the right way, and Your Word says they will not depart from it. I commit _____ to You and trust You to deal with his/her heart and bring him/her home. Work in me. Fill my heart with your peace as I pray and wait.

- *Train up a child in the way he should go: and when he is old, he will not depart from it.*
  Proverbs 22:6 KJV

- *Be persistent in prayer, and keep alert as you pray, giving thanks to God.* **Colossians 4:4 TEV**

Day Three

Lord, forgive me for provoking my children and causing them to feel frustrated. I'm sorry for the times I've been too harsh with them or dealt with them in anger. Help me to think positive thoughts about my children. Help me to look for the best in them and not focus on the negative things I feel, hear, and see. Heal their broken spirits, Lord, and bring each of us back to a place of peace and confidence—in each other and in You.

- *Fathers, do not provoke or irritate or fret your children [do not be hard on them or harass them], lest they become discouraged and sullen and morose and feel inferior and frustrated. [Do not break their spirit.]* **Colossians 3:21 AMP**
- *Restore to me the joy of your salvation and grant me a willing spirit, to sustain me.* **Psalm 51:12 NIV**

Day Four

Father, I thank You—in advance—that my children are walking in the truth. They are obedient, respectful, and do the right thing. Your Word says they will live a long, healthy, and prosperous life on this earth. I pray this in faith, believing in Your promises. I will not be moved by what I see, but will follow your example and call things that are not as though they have already happened.

- *I have no greater joy than to hear my children are walking in the truth.* **3 John 1:4**

- *Children, it is your Christian duty to obey your parents, for this is the right thing to do. Respect your father and mother is the first commandment that has a promise added: so that all may go well with you, and you may live a long time in the land.* **Ephesians 6:1-3 TEV**

- *The God who gives life to the dead and calls things that are not as though they were.* **Romans 4:17 NIV**

Day Five

I belong to You, Lord, and You have covered me with your robe of righteousness. As I strive to honor You with my life, You said my children would be blessed and walk in peace, and I stand upon that promise. Clothe my children with that same robe of righteousness and bless them.

- *The righteous man leads a blameless life; blessed are his children after him.* **Proverbs 20:7 NIV**
- *He has covered me with the robe of righteousness.* **Isaiah 61:10 NKJV**
- *All your children shall be taught by the LORD, and great shall be the peace of your children.* **Isaiah 54:13 NKJV**

Day Six

Thank You, Lord, for the wonderful plan You have for my children. You desire for them to prosper and have a glorious hope and future. I believe with all my heart that You will bring those things to pass and help them fulfill their destiny. You have begun a good work in them and You will be faithful to complete it.

- *For I know the plans I have for you, declares the LORD, plans to prosper you and not to harm you, plans to give you hope and a future.*
Jeremiah 29:11 NIV

- *Being confident of this, that He who began a good work in you will carry it on to completion until the day of Christ Jesus.*
Philippians 1:6 NIV

Day Seven

Father God, I draw close to You today and I thank You for drawing close to me. I submit myself to You—spirit, soul, and body. I resist the devil as You've instructed me to do. Devil, I resist you in the name of Jesus and through His shed blood. I bind your hands and your evil works over this family. You will not torment my mind and you will not have my children.

- *Submit yourselves therefore to God. Resist the devil, and he will flee from you. Draw nigh to God, and He will draw nigh to you.*
James 4:7-8 KJV

- *I tell you the truth, whatever you bind on earth will be bound in heaven, and whatever you loose on earth will be loosed in heaven.* **Matthew 18:18 NIV**

Day Eight

Today I dress myself in the full armor of God so I can stand strong against the devil's schemes and tactics against my children. I clothe myself with the belt of truth, the breastplate of righteousness, and shoes of peace. I take up the shield of faith and put on the helmet of salvation. I wield the sword of the Spirit, the Word of God, which is living and full of power. This is my only offensive weapon against the enemy, and it will rip his plans to shreds.

- *Finally, be strong in the Lord and in His mighty power. Put on the full armor of God so that you can take your stand against the devil's schemes.* **Ephesians 6:10-12 NIV**
- *For the Word of God is living and powerful, and sharper than any two-edged sword.* **Hebrews 4:12 NKJV**

Day Nine

Lord, Your weapons of warfare are not natural, but supernatural. Today, I use those weapons to pull down every stronghold that has set itself against me and my family. I cast down every lie that has exalted itself against our knowledge of You. I take every negative thought that has waged war in my mind and the minds of my children, and bring it captive to the obedience of my Lord, Jesus Christ. I renew my mind with Your Word so I might know Your perfect will.

- *For the weapons of our warfare are not carnal but mighty in God for pulling down strongholds, casting down arguments and every high thing that exalts itself against the knowledge of God, bringing every thought into captivity to the obedience of Christ.* **2 Corinthians 10:4-5 NKJV**

- *And do not be conformed to this world, but be transformed by the renewing of your mind, that you may prove what is that good and acceptable and perfect will of God.* **Romans 12:2 NKJV**

Day Ten

Lord, I thank you that the devil is only *acting* like a ferocious lion—he's all roar and no teeth. His only weapon is deception, and I will not be deceived. Devil, I resist you in the name of Jesus and through His shed blood. Take your hand off my children and stop filling them with your lies.

- *Be self-controlled and alert. Your enemy the devil prowls around like a roaring lion looking for someone to devour. Resist him, standing firm in the faith.* **1 Peter 5:8-9 NIV**
- *For there is no truth in him* (the devil). *When he lies, he speaks his native language, for he is a liar and the father of lies.*
  John 8:44 NIV

Day Eleven

Have mercy and compassion on my children, Lord. Continue to deal with their hearts and help them to forsake their wicked thoughts, words, and deeds. I praise You because You are merciful, long-suffering, and You will abundantly pardon our sin. Great is Your faithfulness.

- *Let the wicked forsake his way, and the unrighteous man his thoughts; let him return to the LORD, And He will have mercy on him; and to our God, for He will abundantly pardon.* **Isaiah 55:7 NKJV**

- *It is of the LORD's mercies that we are not consumed, because His compassions fail not. They are new every morning: great is thy faithfulness.* **Lamentations 3:22-23 KJV**

Day Twelve

Father, I thank You for my children and pray Your hand of protection over them. I plead, invoke, and apply the blood of Jesus over them, spirit, soul, and body. Keep them from the evil one.

- *Just think how much more the blood of Christ will purify our hearts from deeds that lead to death so that we can worship the living God.* **Hebrews 9:14 NLT**

- *But the Lord is faithful, and He will strengthen and protect you from the evil one.* **2 Thessalonians 3:3 NIV**

- *They overcame him by the blood of the Lamb and by the word of their testimony.*
  Revelation 12:11 NIV

Day Thirteen

Angels are a gift from Your hand, Lord, and they hearken to Your Word. I ask for Your angels to continually surround my children and minister to them, for them, and on their behalf. May they prepare the path before my children and keep them from any harm or danger. Be their refuge and fortress. Bring them to Your secret place, that they might always rest and abide under the shadow of the Almighty.

- *For He will command his angels concerning you to guard you in all your ways; they will lift you up in their hands, so that you will not strike your foot against a stone.*
  Psalm 91:11-12 NIV

- *He who dwells in the secret place of the Most High shall abide under the shadow of the Almighty. I will say of the LORD, "He is my refuge and my fortress; my God, in Him I will trust."* **Psalm 91:1-2 NKJV**

Day Fourteen

Lord, you declare in Your Word that no weapon formed against us will prosper—no trap, tactic, or temptation of the enemy. I renounce every lying tongue that has risen against my children. Give them eyes to see, ears to hear, and a heart to understand the truth that You will speak to them by Your Holy Spirit. Help them repent and turn from all evil and detestable practices.

- *No weapon formed against you shall prosper, and every tongue which rises against you in judgment you shall condemn. "This is the heritage of the servants of the LORD, and their righteousness is from Me," says the LORD.*
Isaiah 54:17 NKJV

- *This is what the Sovereign LORD says: "Repent! Turn from your idols and renounce all your detestable practices!"*
Ezekiel 14:6 NIV

Day Fifteen

Father, I thank You in Jesus' name that You have given me power and authority over the works of the enemy. I wash my children in the precious blood of Jesus, and I bind every spirit of conquest, control, and addiction in their lives. May Your Spirit and Your angels minister to my children, bring them home, and restore a right relationship with you.

- *I tell you the truth, whatever you bind on earth will be bound in heaven, and whatever you loose on earth will be loosed in heaven.*
Matthew 18:18 NIV

- *And He called unto Him the twelve, and began to send them forth by two and two; and gave them power over unclean spirits.*
Mark 6:7 KJV

- *And I will do whatever you ask for in my name, so that the Father's glory will be shown through the Son. If you ask me for anything in my name, I will do it.* **John 14:12-14 TEV**

Day Sixteen

Forgive me, Father, where I have failed to discipline my children. Forgive me for the times I have been harsh and corrected them in anger. Help me to set healthy boundaries and not be distracted by their crying, whining, or complaining. Keep me from caving in to their demands.

- *Discipline your children while they are young enough to learn. If you don't, you are helping them destroy themselves.* **Proverbs 19:18 TEV**
- *Chasten thy son while there is hope, and let not thy soul spare for his crying.* **Proverbs 19:18 KJV**
- *Discipline your son, and he will give you peace; he will bring delight to your soul.* **Proverbs 29:17 NIV**

Day Seventeen

Lord, I have taught my children Your Word and Your ways. Your promise is that my children will have great peace and never depart from You. I thank You that my children honor and respect their parents and because of this, they will live a long, healthy, and prosperous life on this earth. I thank You—in spite of the circumstances—that my children are blessed and walking in the truth.

- *All your children shall be taught by the LORD, and great shall be the peace of your children.* **Isaiah 54:13 NKJV**
- *Train up a child in the way he should go: and when he is old, he will not depart from it.* **Proverbs 22:6 KJV**

Day Eighteen

Lord, teach me to use soft answers to turn away anger. Help me to never provoke my children or break their spirit. Let me live a godly lifestyle and always be an example in word and deed. I ask the Holy Spirit to keep watch over my mind and my mouth when I'm tempted to react in the flesh. And help me guard my heart from bitterness, wrong thoughts, and negative emotions.

- *A gentle answer turns away wrath, but a harsh word stirs up anger.* **Proverbs 15:1 NIV**

- *Set a guard over my mouth, O LORD; keep watch over the door of my lips.* **Psalms 141:3 NIV**

Day Nineteen

Father God, Your mighty power is at work in _____, and You can do far more in his/her life than I could even begin to dream, imagine, or dare to ask. I cannot conceive all the things You have prepared for _____, but I thank You for bringing those things to pass. My child's destiny is in Your hand and I believe it will not be sidetracked or stolen.

- *Now glory be to God, who by His mighty power at work within us is able to do far more than we would ever dare to ask or even dream of—infinitely beyond our highest prayers, desires, thoughts, or hopes.* **Ephesians 3:20 TLB**
- *No eye has seen, no ear has heard, no mind has conceived what God has prepared for those who love Him; but God has revealed it to us by His Spirit.* **1 Corinthians 2:9-10 NIV**

Day Twenty

We are surely living in the last days, Lord, and You said You would pour out Your Spirit on all people. I look forward with great expectation to the day when my son/daughter will be filled with Your Spirit, hear Your voice, and prophesy, giving testimony to Your greatness and love.

- *"In the last days," God says, "I will pour out my Spirit on all people. Your sons and daughters will prophesy, your young men will see visions, your old men will dream dreams."* **Acts 2:17 NIV**
- *As bad as you are, you know how to give good things to your children. How much more, then, will the Father in heaven give the Holy Spirit to those who ask Him!* **Luke 11:13 TEV**

Day Twenty-One

Father, I thank You that my children have a deep reverential fear of You, which is the beginning of knowledge. I believe the Holy Spirit is working in them and will guide them back to the right path. My faith confession is that they are not foolish and unwise and do not despise discipline.

- *The fear of the LORD is the beginning of knowledge, but fools despise wisdom and discipline.* **Proverbs 1:7 NIV**
- *A foolish son brings grief to his father and bitterness to the one who bore him.*
  Proverbs 17:25 NIV

Day Twenty-Two

Lord, You said You would never leave, forsake, or abandon us and I believe that applies to my child. May _____ never have to beg for bread or eat with the pigs. Overshadow _____ with Your presence and Your goodness and let him/her know You are as near as their breath.

- *For God has said, "I will never leave you; I will never abandon you."* **Hebrews 13:5 TEV**
- *I was young and now I am old, yet I have never seen the righteous forsaken or their children begging bread.* **Psalm 37:25 NIV**

Day Twenty-Three

Lord, You said when we fear and honor You, we will be successful and You will bless us and our children with Your love and righteousness. Keep my children from disaster. You know their hearts, and I believe they will call out to You and You will answer.

- *The work they do will be successful, and their children will not meet with disaster. I will bless them and their descendants for all time to come. Even before they finish praying to me, I will answer their prayers.* **Isaiah 65:23-24 TEV**
- *But from everlasting to everlasting the LORD's love is with those who fear Him and His righteousness with their children's children.* **Psalm 103:17 NIV**

Day Twenty-Four

Father, Your Word says my children are a gift and a blessing. Help me to see them that way— through Your eyes—no matter how bad things may look in the natural realm. Thank You that they are obedient and pleasing to You.

- *Children are a gift from the LORD; they are a real blessing.* **Psalm 127:3 TEV**
- *Children, obey your parents in everything, for this pleases the Lord.* **Colossians 3:20 NIV**

Day Twenty-Five

I believe my children are attentive to the voice of truth and understanding. Open their eyes, ears, and hearts, and help them to heed sound instruction. Let them hear my voice and the voice of the Shepherd, and never be misled by the voice of a stranger.

- *Sons, listen to what your father teaches you. Pay attention, and you will have understanding. What I am teaching you is good, so remember it all.* **Proverbs 4:1-3 TEV**
- *But they will never follow a stranger; in fact, they will run away from him because they do not recognize a stranger's voice.* **John 10:5 NIV**

Day Twenty-Six

According to Your Word, my children will be mighty in the land. They will be blessed and prosper and their righteousness will endure forever. Thank You that You have a plan and purpose for them, and You will watch over Your Word and perform it on their behalf. When they call upon You, You will hear them and bring them back from their captivity.

- *Blessed is the man who fears the LORD, who finds great delight in His commands. His children will be mighty in the land; the generation of the upright will be blessed. Wealth and riches are in his house, and his righteousness endures forever.* **Psalms 112:1-3 NIV**

- *"For I know the plans I have for you," declares the Lord, "plans to prosper you and not to harm you, plans to give you hope and a future. Then you will call upon me and come and pray to me, and I will listen to you. You will seek me and find me when you seek me with all your heart. I will be found by you," declares the Lord, "and will bring you back from captivity."* **Jeremiah 29:11-14a NIV**

Day Twenty-Seven

Lord, instruct my children and teach them Your ways that are true and right. May they not follow after things that are right in their own eyes. Watch over them and give them godly counsel.

- *I will instruct you and teach you in the way you should go; I will counsel you and watch over you.* **Psalms 32:8 NIV**
- *The way of a fool is right in his own eyes, but he who heeds counsel is wise.* **Proverbs 12:15 NKJV**

Day Twenty-Eight

Father, my children belong to You, and the Spirit of God Who dwells in them is greater than the evil one. I believe my children are victorious over all the works of the enemy and more than conquerors. Nothing on this earth will ever separate them from the love of God in Christ Jesus.

- *You are of God, little children, and have overcome them, because He who is in you is greater than he who is in the world.* **1 John 4:4 NKJV**
- *No, in all these things we are more than conquerors through Him who loved us. For I am convinced that neither death nor life, neither angels nor demons, neither the present nor the future, nor any powers, neither height nor depth, nor anything else in all creation, will be able to separate us from the love of God that is in Christ Jesus our Lord.*
Romans 8:37-39 NIV

Day Twenty-Nine

Thank You, Lord, for dealing with my children every day as a loving father. Encourage them, comfort them, and urge them to live lives worthy of Your great love and mercy. Nothing matters except fearing You, God, and keeping Your commandments. This is my duty and the duty of my children. Continue to work in their hearts. Surround them with Your love and protection. Pour out Your mercy and grace. Keep them close and restore them to a right relationship with You and with their family.

- *For you know that we dealt with each of you as a father deals with his own children, encouraging, comforting and urging you to live lives worthy of God, who calls you into His kingdom and glory.*
  1 Thessalonians 2:11-12 NIV
- *Let us hear the conclusion of the whole matter: Fear God, and keep His commandments: for this is the whole duty of man.*
  Ecclesiastes 12:13 KJV

Day Thirty

Father God, I thank You because all Your words are forever settled in heaven. Your promises are etched in stone. What You have spoken is eternal truth and I can rest in the knowledge that You respond to the prayers of Your children when they seek Your face and stand upon Your Word. Thank You that Your Spirit is drawing my children, the blood of Jesus is cleansing them, and Your angels are continuously watching over them and keeping them from harm. Thank You for Your faithfulness, mercy, and grace. Thank You, most of all, for Your Son, and Your amazing, life-changing, unconditional love.

- *So shall my word be that goes forth from my mouth; it shall not return to me void, but it shall accomplish what I please, and it shall prosper in the thing for which I sent it.* **Isaiah 55:11 NKJV**
- *Forever, O LORD, Your word is settled in heaven. Your faithfulness endures to all generations.* **Psalm 119:89-90 NKJV**
- *God is not a man, that He should lie, nor a son of man, that He should repent. Has He said, and will He not do? Or has He spoken, and will He not make it good?* **Numbers 23:19 NKJV**

Keep the Flame Burning

Now that you have kindled the flame, it's time to keep it burning. Do your own study and look up Scriptures as the Lord leads you. The Bible is filled with truth and promises you can stand on. Keep a journal. Write down your prayers, your feelings, your questions, and your frustrations. When God speaks to your heart or answers a prayer, jot it down. You will be greatly encouraged as you look back over your notes. There is a Personal Journal provided at the end of this book for that purpose.

CHAPTER 5

Words from the Prodigal

W hat better way to end than with words from the prodigals themselves? This chapter will give you advice, suggestions, and even warnings from the prodigal's point of view.

I once asked my daughter what she thought would have happened if her dad had listened to me and put them permanently out of the house. She said, "We might still be out there doing the same old things." For us, *evicting* our kids wasn't the answer, but it may not be the same for you. Every case is different. That's why it's imperative to tune your ear to God's voice and follow His leading. If our children had brought drugs into the house, made a habit of stealing from us, or been physically abusive, it could have been a very different story.

When we're in the middle of our own personal hell, it's difficult to look at things from someone else's perspective—especially those who are causing all the chaos. We correct continually, without considering for even a moment what the other person is thinking or feeling. All we want to do is make the bad behavior go away so we can have peace.

When I asked my children to share ideas for other parents from their perspective, I had no idea what to expect. I was both pleased and surprised at their answers. My daughter said we let them get away with way too much. She went on to say if we had only *threatened* to "shut the door in their faces," they may have rethought their actions a little sooner.

I am thrilled and honored to share their thoughts with you.

Advice from the Prodigal's Point of View

- Give unconditional love, but not to the point of condoning the issues—tough love.

- Wait for your kids to talk to you when they're ready. Don't push. Anything unsolicited a parent says or advises has the potential to drive the child further away. It's natural for someone living in rebellion to push away those they love, and those who love them the most, because—deep down—they are ashamed and will do anything to hide the sin.

- Be open and honest beforehand about things your kids will face—drugs, alcohol, sex, pornography, cigarettes, etc. Help them devise a strategy to deal with those things when the time comes.

- Never be afraid to talk about tough subjects with kids. Kids are smart and inquisitive. If you don't, someone else will. Don't take that chance.

- Don't be afraid of the things your kids are into. Think about your wild side as a kid, and upscale that to how things are now. What was bad when you were young is not the same as what is bad for them. But you can't shelter them from things. If they don't find out from you, they *will* find out from someone.

- Always love on your kids and be affectionate with them. Never wait for them, because that may be what they are doing to you. If you both wait, then you never know where they may go to get that love.

- Encourage and challenge your kids. Don't let them just get by. It may take challenging yourself by spending time with them and finding things for them to do, but that's not a bad idea either. Kids left to themselves, without something constructive to do, get bored and will find something to fill that boredom.

- Never give up on your kids. Always believe in them and let them know you do.

- Never stop loving your kids, even when you don't like them very much. And definitely never stop praying for them. Prayer always works. If you don't know how to pray for them, find someone who will.

- Here is a list of things that will push a rebellious child further away:
    - ✓ Judging, condemning, and causing shame (guilt trip).
    - ✓ Criticizing and constantly finding fault.

- ✓ Threatening—especially empty threats. If you say it, mean it, and stick with it.
- ✓ Being inconsistent with your words, actions, and values.
- ✓ Preaching. Don't tell us—live it and show us.

My Prayer for You

My friend, as you travel this uncertain road, my prayer for you is that, wherever this journey takes you, you are filled with peace, wisdom, and courage. May God hold you and your children in the palm of His hand as He perfects and refines your faith. I believe, with you, that God will truly take what the enemy has meant for evil and destruction and turn it around, working it for your good and His glory. Watch for His hand and listen for His voice.

And never forget … there is *always* hope for the prodigal!

PERSONAL JOURNAL

PERSONAL JOURNAL

PERSONAL JOURNAL

PERSONAL JOURNAL

_____

_____

_____

_____

_____

_____

_____

_____

_____

_____

_____

_____

_____

_____

_____

_____

_____

_____

_____

_____

_____

_____

PERSONAL JOURNAL

A Final Word from the Author ...

Writing this book brought tears and painful memories as I relived many of the events. It also brought about healing and the assurance that my transparency would minister to others going through the same trials and heartache. My sincere prayer is that this book has encouraged you and equipped you to do battle for the souls of your children. God is a God of miracles, healing, and restoration. He is a God of grace, mercy, and provision. He is a God of deliverance and a God of hope. He is a God of love. He *is* love.

If you have your own story to share, or if you would like for someone to pray with you, please drop me a note at andreamerrell7@gmail.com or through my website, www.andreamerrell.com. I would love to hear from you.

If this book has been a blessing to you, please consider posting a review on Amazon. If you know someone who would benefit from *Praying for the Prodigal*, would you help spread the word or purchase a copy for them as a gift?

Thank you. I pray that God will richly bless you and your family in every possible way.

Source Page – Listed by Content Title

1. Chapter One – Definition of a prodigal taken from Merriam-Webster's 11th Collegiate Dictionary.

2. Chapter One – Statistics taken from online source (crosswalk.com/mobile, Carol Barnier) according to the Southern Baptist Council on Family Life.

3. Chapter One – Statistics taken from online source (cbn.com/cbnnews, Paul Strand), 2011 Barna survey.

Made in the USA
Lexington, KY
24 December 2017